The Guide to
ZERO-PROOF COCKTAILS

The Guide to
ZERO-PROOF COCKTAILS

by Sharelle Klaus & Kira Bottles
with Photographs by Joska Borbely
of DRY Soda Company

Contributing Mixologists
Bridgett Bottles, Kira Bottles, Megan Fitzpatrick,
Erik Hakkinen, Amanda Reed, Jermaine Whitehead

CHATWIN BOOKS
Seattle

The Guide to Zero-Proof Cocktails, by Sharelle Klaus & Kira Bottles, with photographs by Joska Borbely, 2020

Photography: Joska Borbely
Cover and book design: Joska Borbely and Annie Brulé

Cover photo recipes appear on pages 164 (front cover) and 151 (back cover).

Printed in Seattle, USA, on FSC certified papers

ISBN 9781633981263

Published by Chatwin Books
www.chatwinbooks.com

Contents

Recipes

Here's to toasting, connecting,
and creating something new together.

Foreword: How It Began

I STARTED DRY FIFTEEN YEARS AGO when I was the mother to four children under the age of seven. I was in the midst of a ten-year period where, because of pregnancies, nursing and general parental responsibilities, I didn't drink. The problem is that as a foodie and an extrovert I love to go to restaurants, parties, and events where the non-alcoholic beverage options would always seem limited to water or Coke. After yet another evening out drinking water with dinner, my entrepreneurial mind started turning. I dreamed about a complex bubbly drink in a beautiful bottle that could pair with food and would make you feel special just holding it.

Once this idea hit, I could think about little else. I brainstormed flavor ideas during my daughter's piano lessons, while nursing my youngest son, and when cooking dinner. There were so many options. My favorite idea, for a lavender beverage, came to me while playing with my kids in the yard. The aroma was so soothing, and I was sure the flavor would be soft and comforting. In my mind it would pair perfectly with chocolate. After I settled on lavender, I chose lemongrass to pair with the Asian flavors I love so much. Then rhubarb, because my grandma used to make

rhubarb pie every summer and I was always amazed by its complexity. Finally, I landed on kumquat because it is my favorite citrus fruit—so unexpected with its sweet peel and sour flesh.

I worked on perfecting these four flavors for hours and hours every day. I tested them on friends and family until they tasted just as I imagined they would. The next step was introducing them to some of Seattle's top restaurants. I brought them samples and had immediate success. The chefs were thrilled to serve a sophisticated non-alcoholic option to their guests; however the sommeliers took a bit of convincing (they were not too keen on talking to a "soda salesperson"). Once I was able to get them to taste it and demonstrate how DRY paired with food, they were sold.

DRY quickly began to grow after I sold it into the first restaurant. We were able to get on the menu of all of Seattle's best restaurants, as well as in our major grocery stores. Shortly thereafter we moved into Los Angeles and San Francisco.

A few months after DRY launched, a pregnant woman sitting next to me on a flight told me about this amazing new drink she had discovered at a friend's dinner party. It was DRY. She talked about how grateful she was to have found a drink that made her feel included. She was quite surprised to hear I was the founder.

I would meet many more people over the years who felt that DRY was created just for them. It was clear that not everyone feels that alcohol needs to be at the center of every celebration or social gathering. Our mission—Social Drinking for Everyone—was becoming more and more relevant.

Today we see a huge shift in how people relate to alcohol. Many are questioning its role in their lives, whether they've stopped drinking it completely or have simply cut back. When I started DRY, I used to beg restaurants to create non-alcoholic menus, and now they're beginning to offer zero-proof cocktails of their own. Mixologists too are challenging themselves to create incredible zero-proof drinks in ways we've never seen before. My fifteen-year-old vision of creating a world where alcohol isn't central to meals or celebrations is becoming reality.

I was inspired to write *The Guide to Zero-Proof Cocktails* for a few reasons: First, I am passionate about making zero-proof drinks the norm, not the exception—the more drinks we create, the better. Second, I love to share recipes, flavors, and drinks I have tried with my friends. Through DRY, I have been blessed to work with some very talented mixologists who have made an array of interesting creations. I wanted to put some of them into a book to share with the world. Finally, I've learned so much over the years from these same mixologists as well as some incredible chefs about how flavors work, and how to create my own recipes, whether in cooking or mixing. This guide includes some of these lessons to inspire creativity and allow everyone to start mixing amazing new drinks on their own.

I want to thank the many amazing people who helped make this guide come to life, from the DRY team to the talented mixologists, to the editor, and to all the champions of DRY. Thank you to Kira Bottles who took this germ of an idea and through sheer force of will and countless late nights turned it into a reality. To Joska Borbely who captured the incredible photography for the book and who partnered with Kira to envision what this guide could be. Thank you to Phil Bevis and Annie Brulé from Chatwin Books for allowing us to publish this book. Thank you to the contributing mixologists who brought such creativity and passion to this project: Bridgett Bottles, Kira Bottles, Megan Fitzpatrick, Erik Hakkinen, Amanda Reed, and Jermaine Whitehead. Thank you to our stylists who helped create the beautiful shots: Callie Meyer and Dawnelle de Marco. To our fearless editor Willa Konsmo, who brought all her talents and skills to helping shape this book. Thank you to the whole team at Why For Good for working with us on this idea each step of the way. And finally, a huge thank you to Betsy Frost, DRY's Chief Marketing Officer for leading this whole process through every idea, edit, meeting, recipe, late night, and photo.

So here is to enjoying this guide. I hope that you try some of these amazing recipes, take inspiration from them, and create your own zero-proof drinks. And most importantly, I hope that you share them at your next celebration.

Cheers,

Sharelle Klaus
CEO & Founder of DRY Soda Company

The *Why* of Zero-Proof

A ZERO-PROOF MOVEMENT IS AFOOT. People are drinking less alcohol than they ever have. While some have stopped drinking entirely, many have simply adopted a more mindful approach to how they consume alcohol, and when. Wherever you fall on the spectrum, the ritual of mixing, presenting, and toasting with something beautiful and delicious without the alcohol should never be treated as a compromise. Zero-proof mixology is a unique experience—rewarding and culinarily rigorous on its own merit.

Alcoholic drinks are no longer the ubiquitous default they once were, and accordingly, a growing number of bars and restaurants have added exciting and innovative zero-proof cocktails to their menus. While we dream of a day where you can simply order a cocktail and be asked if you want it with or without alcohol, the restaurant industry hasn't completely caught up to shifting attitudes. Oftentimes going alcohol-free for the night can feel like a minefield, as many common "mocktails" are overly sweet, overly conspicuous, or overly simple.

Master mixologist Megan Fitzpatrick of Seattle restaurant JuneBaby explained why creating zero-proof beverages with the complexity of a distilled drink is no easy task:

"Often, behind a bar, the only ingredients you have to make zero-proof drinks are syrups, sodas, and juices. These are all equally sugary and sweet! The challenge is to make something complex, and not a sugar bomb. Some of my favorite not-sweet ingredients to play with are teas, vinegars, tinctures, and vegetables."

These options add some of the flavor profiles and complexities of alcohol without the actual booze. While interesting non-alcoholic cocktails are becoming increasingly common, they're not exactly widespread menu staples—yet. To ensure you get the drink you want when eating out, it's useful to check the menu first. Beyond just the drinking experience, the more exposed you are to interesting and complex zero-proof cocktails, and the more you familiarize yourself with your palate, the easier it becomes to experiment on your own.

When mixing zero-proof cocktails at home, knowing what you like is half the battle. The biggest challenge is the lack of booze to anchor a recipe. It can be hard to know where to begin, how to create something balanced, and which ingredients to use. Seattle mixologist Erik Hakkinen of Roquette says:

> "Mixing zero-proof cocktails doesn't have to be trickier. Replacing both the volume and flavor components are your immediate obstacles, in which case your options are either to substitute another flavor or increase those already present. For zero-proof drinks, I like using flavored sodas like DRY, concentrated tea, or tea syrups to add an extra bit of volume and subtle flavor."

We believe that what makes zero-proof mixology difficult also makes it fun. Without the limits on flavor (and cost) of mixing with traditional spirits, a little bit of knowledge around how favors work with one another allows for countless creative combinations.

THE SCIENCE OF TASTING

When discussing zero-proof mixology, it's important to note that flavor and taste are two different words, and they shouldn't be used interchangeably. Taste is one of our five senses, experienced only on the palate. Flavor perception involves, beyond taste, our senses of touch, aroma, and even sight. We can technically only taste five things: sweet, salty, sour, bitter, and umami. But we can perceive the flavor of every ingredient under the sun. We can identify a perfectly ripe summer tomato, for example, or a complex piece of chocolate, or the crispy skin of a roast chicken.

The best zero-proof cocktails are more than just delicious, and they should be as appealing to the eyes as they are to the taste buds. We experience a cocktail with our eyes first, then through smell, and finally with our perception of flavor and texture. So presentation matters. A spectacular glass or a thoughtful garnish will elevate your creation from a simple drink to a cocktail that looks as though it were crafted by a master artist. If a drink looks delicious, studies have shown it will taste more delicious too.

Where there are only five taste sensations, the nose can recognize thousands of fragrances. Scientists agree that 80 to 90 percent of flavor perception is aroma, and this is true more so for certain ingredients than others: vanilla extract, for example, or rosemary, will taste like very little if you're unable to smell it. And aroma acts in much the same way as presentation in that the smell alone sets expectations for how something will taste, and then will actually influence how we perceive that taste.

As you're tasting zero-proof cocktails made by mixologists, or ones that you've made on your own, begin to notice which flavors hit your tongue first, then what you taste as it rests in your mouth, and then the aftertaste. The ability to break down your experience this way will help you better articulate what you like, and it will guide your experimentation. Layering flavors is foundational to building a complex drink.

Equally important is the amount of each taste category you choose to include. It is thought that taste evolved in the human body as a protector or a survival skill. Saltiness indicated there were important mineral nutrients in what was being consumed, and sweetness, similarly, indicated health-promoting nutrients. Bitter foods signaled a poisonous substance that should be avoided, and the perception of sour often suggested that the item being consumed was spoiling or underripe. This explains why today we are still so sensitive to bitter. Even a small amount of a bitter ingredient can quickly become overpowering, whereas it takes a lot of a sugary substance for our palates to detect it at all.

That being said, everyone's palate is unique. Some of us with sweet-tooths can handle a lot of sugar while others who love acidity might find the same amount overwhelming. Some people love olives, for example, while others find the flavor abhorrent. The best judge of whether something tastes good is you, so trust yourself. You never taste something incorrectly; you only experience exactly what your palate detects.

The best way to learn is not through reading, but through experience. So go out and taste, experiment, and tweak, and do it over again. This guide is not simply a recipe book of substitutions for traditional alcoholic drinks, but a foundation for mixing drinks in a completely new way.

According to Seattle mixologist Jermaine Whitehead, the lack of alcohol is what makes zero-proof cocktails so exciting. "The whole experience of the beverage is based solely on the paired flavors within the cocktail," he said. "The possibilities for alcohol-free cocktails are endless."

Welcome to the world of zero-proof!

Flavors

Sweet /swēt/

1. One of the five taste sensations, identified as having the enjoyable perception and pleasing taste of sugar, jam, fruits or honey: not bitter, sour, or salty.

THE MOST COMMON ZERO-PROOF COCKTAIL is sweet. Juices, syrups and sodas are typically what bartenders have on hand, which make them some of the easiest to mix on your own with what's already in your kitchen. Overly sweet "mocktails" may get a bad reputation for being some of the least interesting, but this doesn't have to be the case. Sweet zero-proof cocktails can easily be elevated with a few simple tips.

If sweet is totally your jam, sugar cubes, syrups, honey, fruit, molasses, jam, soda, and cream are all great items to reach for. A professional-level sweet cocktail should still be balanced, and the ingredients complex. For example, plain white granulated sugar is fairly one-note, but using a flavor-infused simple syrup is one of the most effective ways to add complexity to the sweetness. Adding a fruit jam adds brightness and a touch of acidity.

Whatever ingredients you use, the most important thing to keep in mind is that a sweet cocktail should always be balanced and flavorful. Salt, for example, can be one of the best secret weapons when creating a sweet drink: just adding a bit to the rim, or a sprinkle to the mixture before shaken, can amplify its flavors without making it actually taste salty. A sweet zero-proof cocktail should taste like the flavor of its components, but never sugary.

Sour /ˈsou(ə)r/

1. One of the five taste sensations, identified as having an acidic taste that frequently makes the mouth pucker.

SOUR COCKTAILS ARE AMONG the most refreshing and can be some of the most interesting because of the variety of acidic ingredients available. Commonly, sour cocktails lean heavily on citrus, but also consider vinegars, pickled fruits, or shrubs. Apple cider vinegar is the most common choice, for its pleasant fruity kick. If you aren't familiar with shrubs, they're essentially a concentrated syrup of sugar, fruits, and vinegar. Herbs, chilies and spices are often added to the simple fermentation process to add an extra layer of complexity. If you enjoy tart or slightly vinegary drinks, be ready to fall in love.

On the palate, our sour taste receptors are located on the sides of the tongue toward the back of the mouth. Just a whiff of sour foods elicit salivation, and the taste causes a small contraction where these receptors are. The salivation caused by sour drinks provides a sensation of juiciness, even where none is present. To prevent a sour-forward cocktail from becoming unpleasantly acidic, balance the flavor with sweet ingredients, or add a touch of spice for complexity.

As with sweet cocktails, a pinch of salt can make a little sour go a long way. This is why margarita glasses are rimmed with salt, or why a grapefruit tastes more like itself with a light-handed addition.

If you're looking to mix a sour cocktail that's perhaps more interesting than your go-to lime-centric option, try muddling fruits or using their juices for a sweet-sour profile, or opt for pickled vegetables or vinegar-based ingredients for something closer to the savory spectrum.

Bitter /ˈbidər/

1. One of the five taste sensations, identified as having a particularly astringent, pungent, or sharp taste.

BITTER IS PROBABLY THE FLAVOR PROFILE most often overlooked. Use this to your advantage: the skillful addition of a bitter ingredient is among the simplest ways to transform a basic cocktail into something unexpected. Bitter is also unmatched in its ability to tone down sweetness—like that one friend who breaks the tension with a shockingly witty remark among unrelentingly polite company. But that said, bitter is an acquired taste, and just a little too much can throw off the balance of an otherwise harmonious combination.

In the mixology world, tonic water, dark chocolate, unsweetened cocoa, grapefruit juice, and liquid bitters are the usual suspects of the bitter family. Another useful fact to keep in mind when mixing cocktails of any kind is that bitter acts as a palate cleanser. This makes bitter-forward cocktails unexpectedly refreshing, and a good option to serve alongside a rich meal.

A note on liquid bitters: Most bitters are in fact alcoholic, though the small quantity with which they are used doesn't contain enough alcohol for the body to recognize. This book explores a number of ingredients that add bitterness to a drink without using traditional bitters.

Spicy /ˈspīsē/

1. An aromatic or particularly surprising substance with which to flavor food or drinks. Frequently associated with heat or a zingy sensation in the mouth or on the skin.

TECHNICALLY, SPICE ISN'T CONSIDERED one of the major taste categories, but we simply couldn't create a full spectrum of fantastic cocktails without adding spicy drinks to the list. The sensation of spice has far more to do with its burning sensation on our skin (which is sensory), than it does with taste. Chilies are often described as having "heat," even though what feels hot is just the chemical capsaicin, which chilies contain, reacting to the nerve receptors in our mouths.

The general rule for picking chilies is that smaller ones tend to be spicier, and larger ones tend to be milder. Most of the spice from chilies lies in their seeds and pith, so keep them in if you want a little extra spiciness, or leave them out if you're looking for less heat and more flavor. While fresh chilies are an excellent option for muddling, blending, or using as a garnish, dried chilies can pack just as much of a punch, and are perfect for steeping in homemade shrubs or simple syrups.

While important, chilies aren't the only option for adding spice to a cocktail. Spices like cinnamon, nutmeg, cloves, or black pepper evoke a pleasant warmth, rather than a fire. These spices each have their own unique chemical make-ups that produce similar warming effects on the skin or palate.

Spiciness lends itself well to savory profiles (think tomato juice and Tabasco), or to sour—jalapeño with lime, for example, is a classic.

Savory /ˈsāv(ə)rē/

1. One of the five taste sensations, often referred to as salty. Identified as having a well-seasoned or appetizing taste or smell that is not sweet. A balanced salty and herbal flavor.

WHILE FAIRLY UNCOMMON on non-alcoholic menus, a savory zero-proof cocktail can be surprisingly satisfying and complex. Savoriness can be achieved in so many different ways that, with few ingredients, you can mix an unexpected drink with a unique flavor profile.

Without leaning too heavily on alcoholic cocktails for inspiration, we do love the Bloody Mary for its signature combination of olives, onion, salt, bacon, tomato juice, and kosher salt. While it can be difficult to replicate exactly sans-vodka, remember that replication isn't the point. Focusing on balance and on choosing high-quality ingredients will give any traditional Bloody Mary a run for its money.

If you're interested in savory drinks that aren't salt-forward, vegetables and herbs are a subtle way to introduce savory notes. Rosemary is often associated with salty foods, but because it's aromatic, it won't overwhelm the palate. Cucumber, also, is vegetal yet refreshing, and works well balanced with a little bit of sweetness.

Because you aren't spending money on alcohol, we suggest spending it on quality ingredients instead. So pick the freshest herbs, buy the specialty olives (don't forget to keep the brine), and get a variety of salts. Sea salt, kosher, or other specialty salts tend to have a more refined flavor than plain table salt. Olive brine or pickle juice can add acid and salinity. Savory cocktails easily cross the border into the sour category if using vinegar-based ingredients, or into spicy with the addition of chilies or peppercorns— and that's great. The goal, as always, is balance.

Enhancing Flavors

"A turning point for me as far as mixology goes was when I realized the goal isn't to highlight one flavor strongly, but rather to balance flavors across the palate to create something better than the sum of its parts. If you're creating a sweet drink, acid will balance it nicely, and bitterness can add complexity! Anyone can create a drink that tastes like one flavor, but the real fun comes from coming up with a drink that has the flavor profile you're highlighting, but also a few other flavors in harmony at the same time."

—Megan Fitzpatrick, JuneBaby Seattle

To ENHANCE A FLAVOR means to bring out the other central flavors of a beverage or dish.

When one ingredient is used to enhance another, it should be almost undetectable—or at least it should take the back seat. One of the most common enhancing ingredients is salt. Salt enhances sweetness in many of our favorite pairings: think milk chocolate and sea salt, sea salt and watermelon, or prosciutto and melon.

If you've ever forgotten the salt in a cookie recipe, you'll know that the end result tastes dull, flavorless, and somehow less like a cookie. But with the right addition the cookie isn't identifiably salty at all, it just tastes correct.

Learning how to enhance your favorite flavors will take your drinks to the next level. Megan Fitzpatrick said, "I've been using more and more salt in my drinks. I'm so amazed at how much a pinch of salt can emphasize flavors!"

Salt and sugar on their own are common enhancers, and are able to be undetectable because they don't have much flavor of their own besides pure saltiness or sweetness. But don't be afraid to experiment with their more flavorful counterparts, as long as the ingredient you wish to enhance remains the focal point.

As a general rule, salty (or umami) and sweet enhance one another, and sour enhances saltiness.

Balancing Flavors

IF THE GOAL OF ENHANCING FLAVORS is to emphasize, the goal of balancing is to counteract. If a drink or dish tastes too heavily of one flavor—salt, spice, sour, bitter, sweet—you can add a little of something in one of the other taste categories. Just be careful that you're not enhancing a flavor by mistake.

Keep in mind that:

Spicy balances sweet

Sweet balances sour, bitter and spicy

Savory balances bitter

Bitter balances savory

That being said, not every flavor from one category will taste good with every flavor from another, and this is where experimentation comes in.

For example, chilies are delicious, but very one-note on their own. When introduced to a sweet ingredient, like chocolate or fruit, the end result doesn't taste too much of one flavor profile alone.

Complementing Flavors

WHERE *ENHANCING* IS MEANT to bring a single flavor into focus, and *balancing* serves to counteract, *complementing* flavors is all about pairing.

Another way to look at it is that complementing flavors are meant to intensify one another. Achieving a flavor pairing (usually highlighting only two ingredients) is about more than balance, because we're less concerned about the taste category here than we are about the profiles of specific ingredients. You will notice, also, that some of the classic pairings listed here are aromatics, like rosemary or lavender, which would not fall squarely into any particular taste category. Factors such as fat content, texture, and familiarity will also affect the way flavors complement each other.

Take pineapple and coconut as an example: This pairing is successful because coconut has a warm, slightly nutty flavor that is contrasted by pineapple's sweet, acidic punch. Combining pineapple with coconut milk is the more common approach because the milk is fatty and creamy, but using coconut water instead, which is subtler in flavor and is slightly salty, would change the experience. Regardless, pineapple and coconut are so familiarly "tropical," that it's impossible to avoid this comparison, which may or may not be something you want.

While we encourage experimentation, there's nothing wrong with leaning on the classics. We've listed some of our favorites on the next page, but take inspiration from what you eat and drink, and what you see on menus. While pairing flavors successfully is perhaps the most difficult part of creating your own zero-proof recipes—and the reason some flavors work with some things and not others is hard to break down in technical terms—it can also lead to some of the most exciting results.

Our Favorite Flavor Combinations

Lavender and Lemon

Thyme and Grapefruit

Cucumber and Lime

Pineapple and Chili

Lemon and Berry

Chocolate and Vanilla

Berries and Vanilla

Apple and Chai or Cinnamon

Cucumber and Rosemary

Coffee and Lavender

Ginger and Citrus

A Brief Word on Temperature

JUST LIKE IN COOKING, temperature plays a role in mixology. Without alcohol, temperature becomes even more important: Alcohol is inherently astringent, and when added to a mixed cocktail it suppresses the perception of sweetness. Without alcohol, using temperature—either measurable or perceived—is a useful strategy for achieving a similar effect.

For example, most drink recipes that include a bevy of sweet ingredients will suggest that you shake the mixture over ice until it is extremely cold. Coldness suppresses the perception of sweetness. Heat, on the other hand, enhances it. Think of teas, apple ciders, and mixed drinks you might enjoy in the fall and winter: they are typically incredibly sweet. Because you are juxtaposing the temperatures around you with the heat of a drink on your palate, you will perceive these liquids to be sweeter than they are.

Perceived temperature is unique to each palate and can be achieved with different ingredients regardless of measurable temperature. We touched upon this above in discussing how chilies and spices create the perception of heat. But this can work the other way around as well: Some foods, mint in particular, can have a cooling effect. The chemical menthol in the mint leaves creates a perception of cold, which is part of the reason mint teas are popular in hot countries.

Chilies, on the other hand, create the perception of heat on the palate because of the presence of the chemical capsaicin. If you want to add a kick to a drink, even a cold drink, you might add a rim of chili powder, or a chili-infused simple syrup. While the measurable temperature of the beverage may be cold, your palate will perceive the presence of heat. Where you feel this heat on your palate greatly depends on the type of chili you use. Much like the tongue map for the five flavors, different kinds of chilies leave their heat on different parts of the mouth. Commonly used chilies like jalapeños hit at the front of the palate and the tip of the tongue, while cayenne typically affects the front and middle of the tongue, leaving a longer, slower burn.

Tools

Tools

A craftsperson is only as good as their tools.

IMAGINE ASKING A CHEF to prepare perfectly sliced, diced, or julienned ingredients with a butter knife. Imagine asking a painter to expertly blend pigments or add the finishing touches to their art with dried-out bushes. Now imagine asking a bartender to craft a beautifully balanced and tasty drink with just their fingers and an ice cube tray. Sure, everything you asked could probably be done, but the results would be less than refined.

Can you make a drink without bar tools? Yes. But if you want to start making craft zero-proof cocktails at home that impress your friends and yourself, get some good tools!

We've listed the basic tools everyone should own to step up their at-home mixology moments. Don't feel like you have to go buy matching sets if that isn't your aesthetic. The best tools are not only functional but bring style and conversation to your zero-proof partying. We're all for scouring your local vintage shops to find classic and quirky pieces, just make sure you invest in something you will use.

Corkscrew – Pretty self-explanatory. Use this to open bottles of wine or anything with a cork.

Bottle opener – Something to open those Topo Chico bottles or anything that isn't a twist off.

Cocktail shaker – The centerpiece of your bar cart toolkit. There are several kinds of shakers, but we would recommend getting a Boston shaker or a classic all-in-one shaker, sometimes called a cobbler shaker. **A Boston shaker** consists of either two metal tins that fit together, or one metal piece and one glass piece. But unless you have the grip of an NFL wide receiver, we suggest the kind with two metal pieces to avoid glass all over your kitchen floor. **A cobbler shaker** consists of a metal tumbler, a metal lid with a built-in strainer, and a tightly fitting cap. In general, the cobbler shaker is better for beginners as it's less likely to come apart.

Cocktail mixing glass or Yarai – A mixing glass is essentially a short glass pitcher with a lip for pouring. Commonly known as a Yarai, this is a great tool if you prefer your zero-proof martini stirred, not shaken.

Cocktail pitcher – A good cocktail pitcher is typically used for making batch cocktails. They are easily mixed in the pitcher and served at your guests' leisure.

Bar spoon – A bar spoon is no regular spoon. The long handle ensures that you can easily reach the bottom of a pitcher or glass to stir a drink, the flat bowl allows you to create layers, and the twisted shaft allows you to stir without spilling the contents of the glass.

Strainer – There are three basic cocktail strainers worth the investment: The first, a **spring bar strainer,** is the one you will probably use the most, especially if you have a Boston shaker. It fits easily over the top of the metal cup, and the metal spring secures it in place. The second is a **fine mesh strainer,** typically used to strain jams, fruits, or infused syrups. The third is a **julep strainer.** This is *the* classic cocktail strainer, originally used inside julep cups to keep a deluge of ice from hitting your face while drinking. While it's not used for this purpose anymore, it's still a very useful tool for straining larger pieces of herbs, fruit, or ice out of your cocktail mixture.

Jigger – A jigger is a measuring cup designed specifically for bartending. It's usually double-ended and ranges in size between a half-ounce to two and a half ounces. The cups are typically marked on the inside with measuring lines for easy portioning.

Muddler – Much like a pestle, a muddler is used to mash fruits, herbs, and spices in the bottom of a glass or cocktail shaker to release the aromas. The most common muddled cocktail is the mojito, but you will find that muddling is equally as important for creating complexity in zero-proof cocktails.

Peeler – A good peeler can really step up your garnish game. Get a good sharp peeler with a rubber grip to avoid slipping and cutting your hand.

Cocktail picks – A good garnish can make or break the presentation of a drink, and the most efficient way to keep your garnish in place is with a garnish pick. Choose something that suits your style. They can be as simple as a bamboo pick with a knot at the end, or as ornate as a metal pick with a decorative finial. Use them to skewer a few olives for a martini, handle the garnish for a towering Bloody Mary, or for keeping pesky citrus peels in place.

Ice tongs – Ice tongs are just that: tongs with teeth. Use them to pick up slippery little cubes without freezing your fingers. It's more sanitary, and can come in handy if you have particularly delicate Collins glasses.

Large silicone ice cube tray – Okay, now hear us out. Traditional, run-of-the mill ice cube trays are great if you're throwing them into your cocktail shaker to get something cold and frothy. However, if ice is part of your presentation, there is nothing like a perfectly square cube or two in a lovely glass. The silicone ensures crisp edges and easy removal. They come in all shapes and sizes—even spheres! We recommend one that produces a few very large cubes for drinks served in rocks glasses, and one that makes slightly smaller cubes for drinks served in Collins glasses.

Citrus press – A good manual citrus press will make your mixing life so much easier. Citrus is used in a good 90 percent of cocktails, so investing in a good one will save you time and labor in the long run.

Blender – Margaritas anyone? We know it's a controversial topic: Margaritas blended or on the rocks? Even if you are in the "on the rocks" camp, the blender is an important tool for much more than Margaritas. Use it to froth coconut milk, crush ice, or blend herbs to infuse into syrups.

Straws – Straws are important for testing, stirring, and of course drinking. Instead of plastic straws, consider paper, bamboo, stainless steel, or even natural wheat. Pick what works for you and the drinks you like to make, and stock up.

Mixology

Terms to make you sound like a cocktail master.

On the rocks – Over ice.

With a twist – With a citrus peel.

Straight up – Unmixed and unadulterated. More specifically, it means not served on the rocks.

Rim – Adding salt, sugar, spices or some combination to the rim of a cocktail glass. Frequently referenced while making Margaritas. Run some kind of citrus around the rim of a glass and then dip in the salt, sugar or spice mix. If you find the citrus juice isn't holding enough of the salt or sugar, try dipping the rim of the glass in honey instead.

Wheel – This term is frequently used when referring to a garnish. Specifically, a citrus wheel. This means to cut the fruit crosswise to get a thin slice.

Wedge – This garnish is deceptively simple but frequently done wrong. In order to get the perfect citrus wedge, you first must cut the top and the tail off the fruit, then cut the fruit in quarters lengthwise. Ta-da! The perfect wedge.

Neat – Served unmixed, without ice, water or other mixers.

Muddle – To press or crush ingredients against the side and bottom of the glass with a muddling tool. This is most often used for drinks like mojitos where you want to simultaneously break up an herb and release its flavor.

Dirty – To make a drink dirty, you add something to slightly change the color or clarity of the drink. A dirty martini, for example, has added olive juice to make it slightly cloudy and to alter the flavor.

Crushed ice – For all the tropical drink lovers out there. Typically made from small chunks of ice, crushed ice is most commonly used for tropical drinks where you want to filter the ingredients through the small pieces to make it cold. It should also always be served with a straw. No one likes an avalanche of ice on their face.

Cubed ice – We all know what a traditional ice cube looks like and we've experienced that frustrating moment when you go to make a cocktail or ice cold lemonade and someone hasn't refilled that horribly unstable tray. But this kind of cube is best for putting in a shaker and straining out. Use a cube from a silicone mold to serve.

Ice sphere – An ice sphere is just that: a ball of ice typically a bit smaller than a baseball that can be served in a rocks glass with a small amount of liquid. It's really all for presentation, but boy is it effective.

Glassware

Of all the zero-proof gin joints...

A COCKTAIL GLASS is more than just a pretty accessory. The ritual of using the right glassware can change the drinking experience. A champagne toast is not the same with a water glass. Besides presentation, using the correct glassware enhances the sensory experience. For example, the coupe, which was traditionally used to serve champagne, works best for chilled, aromatic drinks. Your choice of glassware can be just as important as flavor and technique when making and serving zero-proof cocktails.

Rocks or Lowball Glass

8 to 10 fluid ounces

A rocks glass, also called a lowball, is on the shorter side with a heavier base. It's ideal for anything you might want to drink neat, or with one or two ice cubes. Typically, these glasses are not meant to be filled to the very top. At most, they're filled about halfway. Traditionally used for drinks like the Old Fashioned, whiskey on the rocks, and scotch and soda, they are a bar cart must-have. With the variety of high quality zero-proof liquor now on the market, we recommend using these glasses for the 1890, our take on an Old Fashioned, or a zero-proof whiskey and soda.

Collins or Highball Glass

8 to 12 fluid ounces for a highball
12 to 16 fluid ounces for a Collins

The highball is a great, versatile glass with a distinctive tall, cylindrical shape. Traditionally used for drinks like gin & tonics and whiskey highballs, these glasses are equally as important to have on hand for making zero-proof cocktails. They are a go-to for simple mixed drinks of two, maybe three ingredients on ice. They can also be repurposed as a tiki glass for drinks served over crushed ice.

Martini Glass

5 to 8 fluid ounces

Contrary to popular belief, the martini glass wasn't a child of the jazz age. It was invented sometime in the 19th century because of the lack of readily available ice. The drinks they hold are meant to be served chilled, and the long stem allows the drink to remain cold and away from warm hands. The only real downside to the martini glass is that if you don't have a steady hand, your drink may end up on the person sitting across from you. Besides the fact that they spill easily, the only difference between a martini and a coupe glass is aesthetic. So if you are going to invest in only one of these glasses, we suggest you go with your favorite style.

Coupe

5 to 7 fluid ounces

Although originally designed to serve sparkling wine, coupe glasses are better suited for non-bubbly drinks. The large diameter of the mouth creates more opportunities for bubbles to escape, as opposed to a glass with a smaller opening and taller sides. Bartenders we've talked to prefer them to martini glasses because they don't spill as easily. Coupe glasses are great for aromatic drinks, so use them for simple recipes with an herbal garnish, or for aromatic-forward mixed drinks.

Champagne Flute

6 fluid ounces

Champagne flutes became popular in the mid-1950s because the tall, narrow shape helped sparkling wines retain their bubbles, and the long shape is thought to send delicate aromas up toward the nose. We recommend serving chilled, bubbly drinks in champagne flutes, but keep in mind that if you're serving a bold, aromatic cocktail a glass with a wider mouth like a coupe or martini glass may be a better option.

Wine Glasses

12 to 14 fluid ounces for red wine glasses
8 to 12 fluid ounces for white wine glasses

Not all wine glasses are created equal. There are a variety of shapes and sizes on the market, but for a basic bar cart setup, either simple white or red wine glasses work just fine. Red wine glasses are typically larger and more bulbous in shape, to allow space for the wines to breathe and release their aromas. White wine glasses are smaller, with narrower openings. The smaller mouth preserves their more delicate aromas, and the small size ensures the chilled wine doesn't get warm too quickly. For our purposes, either of these would work, but we recommend red wine glasses for more full bodied drinks like our zero-proof sangria, and white wine glasses for more delicate drinks like the PNW Breeze. If you prefer to invest in one style over the other, we recommend considering the drinks you think you will make the most and choosing the size accordingly.

Stocking a Bar Cart (Supplies)

When life gives you lemons…Put them on a bar cart.

Whether stocking your bar cart for a party of many or a party of one, there are a few essentials to keep on hand. We've put together a basic list based on the recipes in this book to help you navigate the many available options.

Mixers:

Juices

- Lemon juice
- Lime juice
- Grapefruit juice
- Cranberry juice
- Orange juice
- Pineapple juice

Bitters

- Angostura bitters
- Orange bitters
- Cocoa bitters
- Rhubarb bitters
- Grapefruit bitters

Simple Syrups

A few of our favorites from Portland Syrups:
- Bright Chai
- Vanilla Spice Rooibos
- Habañero Mango
- Spicy Ginger
- Marionberry

Shrubs

A few of our favorites from Element Shrub:
- Blood Orange Saffron
- Lemon Mint
- Honeydew Jalapeño

Other Things:

Grenadine

Garnishes

Fruit
- Citrus fruits like lemons, limes, grapefruits and blood oranges
- Berries like blueberries, strawberries, raspberries and blackberries
- Canned cherries like basic maraschino or the more elegant Luxardo

Olives—Typically green, buttery olives like Castelvetranos

Pickles—Small cornichons, dill, spicy and sweet are all great options, as are pickled vegetables such as pickled bell peppers and chilies

Chilies—Fresh jalapeños and serranos, as well as dried red chilies (like chiles de árbol)

Sugar Cubes—Both white and brown

Salt—Kosher and table

Spices—Cinnamon (sticks and ground), chipotle, chili powder and nutmeg

Herbs—Fresh rosemary, thyme, mint, sage, basil and dried lavender

Fresh ginger

A Syrup So Simple

SIMPLE SYRUP IS A COMMON cocktail ingredient, zero-proof or otherwise. Unlike the masses of "simple" recipes that are actually complex, we are happy to report that this is indeed a simple recipe. It's equal parts sugar and water, which is about as straightforward as it gets. You might be wondering why you wouldn't just add sugar to a recipe that calls for simple syrup. While we are all for simplicity, there are a few reasons to take the time to make it.

First off, heating sugar in water changes its molecular structure, which produces a viscous liquid that is silky in texture and readily dissolves into your cocktails. Turning the sugar into a liquid also means it can be measured in a jigger along with the other liquids in your beverage. It also creates density that allows for the separation of layers. The rule for creating perfectly separated layers in any drink means starting with the heaviest liquid, which is always the liquid with the most sugar. Sugar on its own can do none of this, and will typically result in undissolved granules sunk to the bottom of your glass.

Second, simple syrup can be a fantastic flavor carrier. Because this recipe involves liquid and heat, you have the opportunity to infuse the syrup with aromatics like lavender buds or dried chilies. We've included the basic recipe here, along with some of our favorite infusions.

Basic Simple Syrup

1 cup granulated sugar
1 cup water

Combine the water and sugar in a saucepan over medium heat, stirring periodically until the sugar dissolves. Bring to a gentle boil, and immediately take off the heat. Let it cool to room temperature, then strain into a glass jar. Store in the refrigerator, tightly sealed for up to one month.

Chili Simple Syrup

1 cup granulated sugar
1 cup water
6–10 dried chiles de árbol

Combine the water and sugar in a saucepan over medium heat, stirring periodically until the sugar dissolves. Bring to a gentle boil, and immediately take off the heat. Place the dried chilies in a heat-proof bowl, pour in the hot syrup mixture, and let steep until cool, then strain into a glass jar. Discard the chilies. Store in the refrigerator for up to one month.

Lavender Simple Syrup

1 cup granulated sugar
1 cup water
¼ cup dried lavender buds

Combine the water and sugar in a saucepan over medium heat, stirring periodically until the sugar dissolves. Bring to a gentle boil, and immediately take off the heat. Place the dried lavender buds in a heat-proof bowl, pour in the hot syrup mixture, let steep until cool, then strain into a glass jar. Discard the buds. Store in the refrigerator for up to one month.

Ginger Simple Syrup

1 cup granulated sugar

1 cup water

*¼ cup fresh ginger root, peeled and
  roughly chopped*

Combine the water and sugar in a
saucepan over medium heat, stirring
periodically until the sugar dissolves.
Bring to a gentle boil, and immediately
take off the heat. Place the ginger root in
a heat-proof bowl, pour in the hot syrup
mixture, let steep until cool, then strain
into a glass jar. Discard the ginger. Store
in the refrigerator for up to one month.

Ginger & Serrano Chili Simple Syrup

1 cup granulated sugar

1 cup water

*¼ cup fresh ginger root, peeled and
  roughly chopped*

*1 serrano chili, stem removed and
  roughly chopped (best to wear
  latex gloves when handling chilies)*

Combine the water and sugar in a
saucepan over medium heat, stirring
periodically until the sugar dissolves.
Bring to a gentle boil, and immediately
take off the heat. Place the ginger root
and chili in a heat-proof bowl, pour
in the hot syrup mixture, let steep
until cool, then strain into a glass jar.
Discard the ginger and chili. Store in the
refrigerator for up to one month.

*Check out these recipes to see how to incorporate
simple syrups into your drinks:*

Soda and Syrup, p. 59

Soda and Chili, p. 124

Short and Sassy, p. 127

Smoke and Mirrors, p. 139

Beet It, p. 160

Sweet

Soda & Syrup

1 oz. flavored simple syrup (see recipes p. 52)
7 oz. club soda

Place ice in a rocks glass and add the syrup of your choice, top with club soda, and garnish with anything that complements your syrup.

Garnish: Any garnish to complement your syrup

Glass: Rocks glass

Basic Simple Syrup

1 cup granulated sugar
1 cup water

Combine the water and sugar in a saucepan and heat on the stove until the sugar has dissolved, stirring periodically. Bring to a boil and immediately take off the heat. If you want to flavor your syrup, place items like fresh mint, orange peel, vanilla pods, or lavender into a heat-proof bowl and pour over the hot syrup mixture. Let steep until cool. Once cool, strain the mixture into a glass jar. Discard the flavoring items. Keep in the refrigerator for up to a month.

Flamingle

1½ oz. Lyre's Aperitif Rosso
½ oz. lemon juice
6 oz. DRY Blood Orange Botanical Bubbly

In a rocks glass add one large ice cube. Pour in the lemon juice and Lyre's Aperitif Rosso, and top with the DRY Blood Orange Botanical Bubbly. Garnish with a lemon twist.

Garnish: Lemon twist

Glass: Rocks glass

This drink is the perfect example of how a few well-balanced ingredients can make a truly amazing cocktail. You'll spend your time mingling (or should we say flamingling) instead of painstakingly mixing the perfect cocktail with a million ingredients.

Mom-osa

4 oz. DRY Botanical Bubbly in your favorite
   flavor, chilled
4 oz. orange juice

Simply pour DRY Botanical Bubbly into your glass,
then add the orange juice. Garnish with your favorite
berries, mint or edible flowers.

Garnish: Berries, mint, or edible flowers

Glass: Martini glass or champagne flute

*This recipe is our ode to mammas-to-be.
Our classic recipe uses DRY Lavender
Botanical Bubbly, and if you want to kick it
up a notch, rim the glass with a little honey
and dip it into dried lavender buds.*

*This recipe also works well with different
kinds of juice, different flavors of our
bubbly, or even club soda. Try grapefruit
juice with DRY Blood Orange Botanical
Bubbly, or a tropical mix of passion fruit
juice and DRY Pineapple Botanical Bubbly
for a vacation in a glass.*

1890

1 sugar cube

½ tsp. maraschino cherry syrup

2–3 dashes orange bitters

¼ oz. Vanilla Spice Rooibos Syrup by Portland Syrups

1 Cara Cara orange slice

1 oz. zero-proof whiskey

5 oz. club soda

In a glass add sugar cube, bitters, maraschino cherry syrup, vanilla spice syrup, zero-proof whiskey and orange slice. Muddle until the sugar cube has dissolved and the orange slice is well incorporated. Add ice and club soda. Stir until mixed and very cold. Strain into a coupe and garnish with an orange peel and cherry.

Garnish: Orange peel and a cherry

Glass: Coupe or rocks glass

If you like things a little sweeter and less fizzy, you can add a splash of fresh Cara Cara orange juice or DRY Blood Orange Botanical Bubbly in place of the club soda. This drink gets its name from the origins of its inspiration: the Old Fashioned. Thought to have been developed in Kentucky in the late 1880s to early 1890s, it's one of the most popular classic cocktails.

DRY Fuji Apple Fall Sangria

By Jermaine Whitehead

1½ oz. pomegranate juice (such as POM)
1 oz. hibiscus syrup (see recipe below)
1 oz. water
¾ oz. lime juice
¼ oz. orange juice
DRY Fuji Apple Botanical Bubbly

Add pomegranate juice, hibiscus syrup, water, lime juice and orange juice to a shaker. Shake and strain into a wine glass. Top with DRY Fuji Apple Botanical Bubbly. Garnish with lime wheels, lemon wheels, orange wheels, and fresh mint.

Garnish: Lime wheel

Glass: Wine glass

Hibiscus Syrup

1 cup sugar
½ cup water
2 hibiscus tea bags
1 tsp. cinnamon powder
2 drops orange flower water

Add sugar and water to a pot and bring to a gentle boil. Add cinnamon, orange flower water, and tea bags. Turn off heat and let steep for 5 minutes. Strain.

Float On

1–2 scoops ice cream or sorbet
Club soda or DRY Botanical Bubbly

In your favorite fancy glass, scoop one or two scoops of ice cream or sorbet and top with either club soda or DRY Botanical Bubbly.

We know this sounds like a dessert, but hear us out: Many cocktails are made with muddled fruit, simple syrup, ice, or cream, so really there isn't much of a difference between that and making a really sophisticated float into a beautiful cocktail.

Garnish: Fresh mint or rosemary

Glass: Coupe or martini glass

A few of our favorite combos:

1 scoop mango sorbet topped with club soda and a dash of orange bitters.

1 scoop coconut sorbet topped with club soda and fresh mint or rosemary.

1 scoop mint chocolate chip ice cream topped with DRY Vanilla Botanical Bubbly.

1 scoop mint or coconut sorbet topped with DRY Lavender Botanical Bubbly and fresh mint.

Tiki Bird

1½ oz. Lyre's American Malt
½ tsp. real maple syrup
1 dash aromatic bitters
1 oz. pineapple juice (canned is fine)
1 tsp. maraschino cherry syrup
Squeeze of lemon juice
4 oz. club soda or DRY Pineapple Botanical
  Bubbly

Fill a highball or Collins glass with crushed ice. Pour over Lyre's American Malt, maple syrup, bitters, pineapple juice, cherry syrup, and lemon juice to taste. Top with club soda if you like a milder, less sweet flavor. For a tropical twist, top with DRY Pineapple Botanical Bubbly. Garnish with pineapple chunks and a cherry on a pick, and a tropical leaf for some added style.

Garnish: Pineapple chunks and a cherry on a pick

Glass: Collins or highball glass

Zero-Proof Blushing Bee's Knees

½ oz. lemon juice
Raspberries
1 tsp. honey
6 oz. DRY Vanilla Botanical Bubbly

Add lemon juice, 3 raspberries, honey, and a dash of water to a cocktail shaker, and shake until combined. Strain the mixture into a glass, and top with DRY Vanilla Botanical Bubbly. Garnish with raspberries.

Garnish: Raspberries

Glass: Coupe

Add a scoop of raspberry sorbet to make this Prohibition-era drink extra special.

DRY Vanilla Pumpkin Spice Latte

By Jermaine Whitehead

1½ oz. water
1½ oz. espresso
½ oz. simple syrup (see recipe on p. 52)
½ oz. egg white (optional)
½ oz. pumpkin spice creamer
DRY Vanilla Botanical Bubbly

In a cocktail shaker add water, espresso, simple syrup, egg white, pumpkin spice creamer and ice. Shake vigorously until cold and strain into an ice-filled glass. Top with DRY Vanilla Botanical Bubbly. Garnish with edible flowers and fresh grated cinnamon.

Garnish: Edible flowers

Glass: Wine glass or rocks glass

Note regarding egg whites: *Consuming* **raw or undercooked eggs** *may increase your risk of foodborne illness. Do so at your own risk.*

Upside Down DRY

1 Tbsp. pineapple juice
2 oz. unsweetened coconut milk
6 oz. DRY Pineapple Botanical Bubbly
1 oz. maraschino cherry syrup

In a shaker add ice, pineapple juice and coconut milk and shake until cold and frothy. Pour into a lowball glass and top with DRY Pineapple Botanical Bubbly. Spoon maraschino cherry juice gently and evenly over the top, and garnish with a maraschino cherry and pineapple wheel.

Garnish: Pineapple wheel and a cherry

Glass: Rocks glass

Sour

Soda & Shrubs

½–1 oz. shrubs
5–7 oz. club soda

In a rocks glass, add ice, shrubs of your choice, and club soda. Garnish with a citrus peel or fruit wedge that complements the flavor of your shrubs.

Garnish: Citrus peel or fruit wedge

Glass: Rocks glass

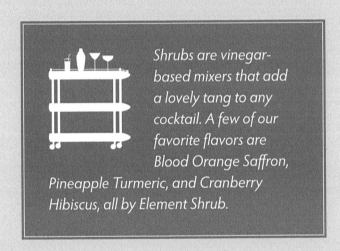

Shrubs are vinegar-based mixers that add a lovely tang to any cocktail. A few of our favorite flavors are Blood Orange Saffron, Pineapple Turmeric, and Cranberry Hibiscus, all by Element Shrub.

Blueberry Lavender Lemonade

Blueberries
4 oz. lemonade
4 oz. DRY Lavender Botanical Bubbly

Drop a few fresh blueberries in the bottom of a glass, add lemonade and then top with DRY Lavender Botanical Bubbly. Garnish with a lemon peel.

Garnish: Lemon peel and blueberries

Glass: Collins glass

This is our classic summer favorite. Easy, elegant, and oh so delicious. We highly recommend mixing this drink for a baby shower, summer brunch with friends, or even an afternoon business lunch.

DRY Gimlet

1 oz. Seedlip Garden 108 Non-Alcoholic Spirit
1 oz. lime juice
7 oz. DRY Cucumber Botanical Bubbly, chilled

In a coupe or martini glass, mix Seedlip Garden 108 and lime juice. Top with very cold DRY Cucumber Botanical Bubbly. Garnish with a lime wedge.

Garnish: Lime wedge

Glass: Coupe or martini glass

Watermelon Spritz

Lime wedge
Kosher salt
½ oz. Lemon Mint Shrub by Element Shrub
6 oz. DRY Watermelon Botanical Bubbly

Rim a rocks glass by running a lime wedge around the edge of your glass and dipping into kosher salt. Place one big ice cube in the glass and pour Lemon Mint Shrub over the ice. Top with very cold DRY Watermelon Botanical Bubbly. Garnish with a lime wheel.

Garnish: Lime wheel

Glass: Rocks glass

This drink tastes like a super sophisticated sour watermelon candy. You know the one. We recommend enjoying this on a hot day, in the sun, with a breeze.

PNW Breeze

6 oz. DRY Lavender Botanical Bubbly
1 oz. lemon juice
1 oz. Marionberry Syrup by Portland Syrups

In a wine glass or rocks glass add very cold DRY Lavender Botanical Bubbly and lemon juice. Drizzle in Marionberry Syrup over the back of a bar spoon. If done gently and correctly, the colors should separate. Garnish with a blackberry wrapped in a lemon peel secured with a cocktail pick.

Garnish: Blackberry wrapped in lemon peel

Glass: Wine glass or rocks glass

Sour Apple Spritz

by Amanda Reed

4 oz. DRY Fuji Apple Botanical Bubbly
2 oz. white verjus (verjus is the fresh juice of un-
ripe wine grapes)
½ oz. cinnamon-demerara (see recipe below)

Add ingredients to a Collins glass and mix. Garnish with an apple slice.

Garnish: Dried or fresh apple slice

Glass: Collins glass

Cinnamon-Demerara

8 oz. demerara sugar
8 oz. water
2 cinnamon sticks

Combine sugar and water in a saucepan and heat until sugar dissolves. Add cinnamon and infuse for 48 hours. Pour through a fine mesh strainer.

Blood Orange Sour

by Erik Hakkinen of Roquette

½ oz. orgeat syrup
½ oz. cinnamon syrup (see recipe below)
1 oz. sour orange juice (juice from 2 oranges, 1
   lime, 1 lemon)
4–5 oz. DRY Blood Orange Botanical Bubbly

In a cocktail shaker add ice, both syrups, and the sour orange juice. Shake until cold and strain into a rocks glass. Top with DRY Blood Orange Botanical Bubbly. If you like your drinks on ice, feel free to add it, but we find that if you shake the mixture until cold, you won't need it. Garnish with a fresh orange slice.

Garnish: Orange slice

Glass: Rocks glass

Cinnamon Syrup

1 cup granulated sugar
1 cup water
2–3 crushed cinnamon sticks

Combine the water and sugar in a saucepan and heat until the sugar has dissolved, stirring periodically. Bring to a boil and immediately take off the heat and add the cinnamon sticks to steep. Let the mixture cool to room temperature. Once cool, strain the mixture into a glass jar. Keep in the refrigerator for up to a month, tightly sealed.

Gatsby's Garden

1 oz. lemon juice
1 oz. zero-proof gin
1 sugar cube
2–3 dashes orange bitters
6 oz. DRY Lavender Botanical Bubbly

In a cocktail shaker add ice, lemon juice, sugar cube, zero-proof gin, and orange bitters. Stir until cold, and strain into a coupe glass. Top with 6 oz. DRY Lavender Botanical Bubbly and garnish with a lemon twist.

Garnish: Lemon twist

Glass: Coupe

The DRY 75

1 sugar cube
2–3 dashes bitters (optional)
1 oz. lemon juice
½ oz. zero-proof gin
6 oz. DRY Ginger Botanical Bubbly

Add sugar cube and bitters to a shaker, and let the bitters be absorbed by the cube. Smash the sugar cube and add lemon juice and zero-proof gin. Shake until very cold and frothy. Pour into a champagne flute or coupe, and top with DRY Ginger Botanical Bubbly. Garnish with a lemon twist on the edge.

Garnish: Lemon twist

Glass: Champagne flute or coupe

Strawberry Kisses

3–4 strawberries, sliced
1 sugar cube
½ oz. Honeydew Jalapeño Shrub by Element Shrub
1 tsp. pineapple juice
7 oz. club soda or DRY Pineapple Botanical Bubbly

In a cocktail shaker, muddle strawberries and sugar cube. Add Honeydew Jalapeño Shrub and muddle again. In a Collins glass add ice and pour in the strawberry mixture. Top with pineapple juice and DRY Pineapple Botanical Bubbly. Garnish with a strawberry slice and straw.

Garnish: Strawberry slice and a straw

Glass: Collins glass

Bitter

Bitters & Soda

2–3 dashes bitters in a flavor of your choice
6–8 oz. club soda or tonic

In a rocks glass place one large ice cube or sphere. Top with soda or tonic and add a few dashes of bitters. Garnish with a citrus peel, rhubarb ribbon, or fresh herbs to complement your flavor choice.

Garnish: Citrus peel, rhubarb ribbon or herb sprig

Glass: Rocks glass

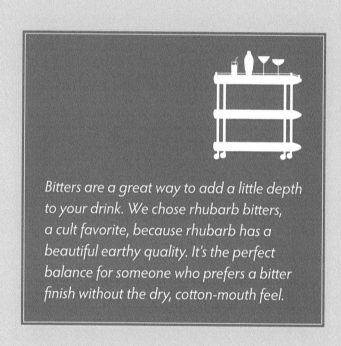

Bitters are a great way to add a little depth to your drink. We chose rhubarb bitters, a cult favorite, because rhubarb has a beautiful earthy quality. It's the perfect balance for someone who prefers a bitter finish without the dry, cotton-mouth feel.

North Americano

By Erik Hakkinen of Roquette

1 oz. Lyre's Aperitif Rosso
½ oz. Giffard Aperitif Syrup
6 oz. DRY Blood Orange Botanical Bubbly

In a chilled Collins or tumbler glass add Lyre's Aperitif Rosso and Giffard Aperitif Syrup. Stir gently to incorporate. Add 2 oz. DRY Blood Orange Botanical Bubbly, then add ice. Top with remaining DRY Botanical Bubbly, and garnish with a halved orange slice.

Garnish: Halved orange slice

Glass: Collins or tumbler, chilled

Simple Paloma

½ oz. lime juice and extra lime wedge
1 oz. grapefruit juice
Kosher salt
6 oz. DRY Blood Orange Botanical Bubbly

In a cocktail shaker, combine lime and grapefruit juice with ice and shake until cold. Rim a Collins or highball glass with a lime wedge and kosher salt, and add ice. Strain juice mixture into the glass and top with DRY Blood Orange Botanical Bubbly. Garnish with a lime wheel.

Garnish: Lime wheel

Glass: Collins, highball or rocks glass

This classic summer drink is—dare we say—even more delicious in its zero-proof form. If you find that lime juice isn't quite sticky enough to get your salt to stick to the rim, use honey. Pour a small amount of honey onto a plate and let it spread. Dip the rim of your empty glass into the honey and then into the salt. We recommend skipping the straw on this drink, to get a little bit of salt with each sip.

Ginger Lime Mule

By Erik Hakkinen of Roquette

8–10 mint leaves
½ oz. lime juice
DRY Ginger Botanical Bubbly
½ oz. simple syrup (optional—see recipe p. 52)

In a cocktail shaker add the mint leaves, lime juice and simple syrup. Lightly muddle together. Pour the muddled mixture over ice in a Collins glass. Top with DRY Ginger Botanical Bubbly and stir gently. Garnish with mint leaves, lime peel and a straw.

Garnish: Mint leaves and lime peel

Glass: Collins glass

Vanilla Grapefruit Fizz

Grapefruit juice
DRY Vanilla Botanical Bubbly

Fill a highball glass ¾ of the way full with grapefruit juice and top with DRY Vanilla Botanical Bubbly. Garnish with a wedge of grapefruit and a sprig of mint.

Garnish: Grapefruit wedge and mint

Glass: Highball glass

Bitter Bella

by Amanda Reed

3 oz. DRY Blood Orange Botanical Bubbly
¾ oz. grenadine (see recipe below)
1½ oz. fresh lime juice
1 dash Fee Brothers Aromatic Bitters

Combine all ingredients in a shaker with ice. Shake and strain into a coupe glass. Garnish with a lime wheel.

Garnish: Lime wheel, dehydrated or fresh

Glass: Coupe

Grenadine

6 oz. pomegranate juice
6 oz. sugar
1 oz. pomegranate molasses

Combine all ingredients in a saucepan. Heat until sugar dissolves.

Grapefruit Rag-Thyme

3 oz. ruby red grapefruit juice
1 sprig of fresh thyme
1 sugar cube
5 oz. DRY Ginger Botanical Bubbly

In a cocktail shaker combine grapefruit juice, thyme leaves, sugar cube and ice. Shake until cold. It's best to be very vigorous in your shaking, as you want the sugar cube to dissolve completely. Strain into a coupe or wine glass. Top with DRY Ginger Botanical Bubbly. Garnish with a thick slice of grapefruit and a sprig of thyme.

Garnish: Grapefruit slice and thyme

Glass: Wine glass or coupe

Sparkly Dog

by Megan Fitzpatrick of JuneBaby

Grapefruit Cordial

1½ oz. simple syrup
1½ oz. grapefruit juice
Peels of one grapefruit

Combine grapefruit juice, simple syrup, and grapefruit peels in a small pot and simmer over medium heat for 12 minutes. Remove from heat and strain.

Grapefruit and salt came together during the first and second World Wars, when sugar was rationed and grapefruit sales plummeted. Salt manufacturers and grapefruit growers teamed up to push their products together. Salt inhibits taste buds from perceiving bitterness, so salt enhances a grapefruit's sweetness without the addition of sugar. This is still a regional practice in the South.

3 oz. grapefruit cordial (see recipe at left)
½ oz. lime juice
¼ oz. saline solution (5 parts water to 1 part salt)
2 oz. club soda

Combine the grapefruit cordial, lime juice, and saline solution in a shaker. Shake and strain into a Collins glass. Top with club soda and fill with ice. Garnish with a lime wheel.

Garnish: Lime wheel

Glass: Collins glass

Another Round of Strawberry for Me and My Friends

by Megan Fitzpatrick of Junebaby

½ oz. strawberry syrup (see recipe at right)
½ oz. rooibos tea tincture (see recipe below)
¼ oz. lemon juice
2 oz. DRY Vanilla Botanical Bubbly

Combine all ingredients in a rocks glass and stir. Fill the glass with ice and garnish with fresh mint leaves.

Garnish: Mint leaves

Glass: Rocks glass

Rooibos Tea Tincture

Rooibos tea leaves

Steep 1 part rooibos tea leaves in 5 parts boiling water. You cannot over-steep this; you want the bitterness of the tannins to come through. Let it steep until cool, and strain.

Strawberry Syrup

1 lb. strawberries
1 cup sugar

For the strawberry syrup, dice your strawberries and combine with the sugar in a bowl. Give them a good mash. Let sit on your counter for three days covered with a dish towel secured with a rubber band, stirring each day. Strain and press the solids to extract as much liquid as possible. We've included several hot process syrup recipes at the beginning of this book, but in this case we prefer the cold process. It ends up less jammy, and the fruit flavor tastes truer to its intended form.

Coffee Cha-Cha

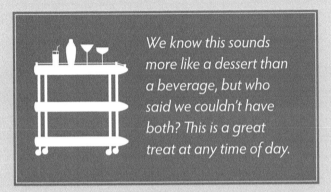

We know this sounds more like a dessert than a beverage, but who said we couldn't have both? This is a great treat at any time of day.

1 Tbsp. hot water

1 Tbsp. sugar

1 Tbsp. instant coffee or espresso (depending on your coffee preference)

½ oz. milk of your choice (we recommend coconut milk or 2% milk: the higher fat content makes a better blend)

1 tsp. cinnamon

1 tsp. chocolate syrup

4 oz. DRY Vanilla Botanical Bubbly

In a bowl, add hot water, sugar, and instant coffee. Using a hand-held mixer, whisk until stiff peaks form. This takes about 8 minutes. Once the peaks form, add the cinnamon and whisk to incorporate.
In a martini glass, add chocolate syrup and gently turn the glass to evenly coat the sides. Spoon in about ½ cup of the whipped coffee. On one side of the glass, gently pour in the milk and follow with DRY Vanilla Botanical Bubbly. Top with a dash of cinnamon and a chocolate espresso bean.

Garnish: Chocolate espresso bean

Glass: Martini glass

Spicy

Soda & Chili

1 oz. chili simple syrup (see recipe below)
5–7 oz. club soda

Place one large ice cube in a rocks glass and add the simple syrup. Top with club soda and garnish with a dried chili.

Garnish: Dried chili

Glass: Rocks glass

Chili Simple Syrup

1 cup granulated sugar
1 cup water
6–10 dried chiles de árbol

Combine the water and sugar in a saucepan and heat until the sugar has dissolved, stirring periodically. Bring to a boil and immediately take off the heat. Place the dried chilies in a heat-proof bowl, pour over the hot syrup mixture and let this steep until cool. Once cool, strain the mixture into a glass jar. Discard the chilies. Keep in the refrigerator for up to one month.

Short & Sassy

1 oz. ginger syrup (recipe below)
2 oz. Lyre's American Malt
3–5 oz. club soda

In a rocks glass add ice, simple syrup and Lyre's American Malt. Top with club soda and garnish with a citrus peel or a wedge of fresh ginger root.

Garnish: Citrus peel or fresh ginger

Glass: Rocks glass

Ginger Simple Syrup

1 cup granulated sugar
1 cup water
3-inch piece of fresh ginger root,
peeled, sliced and lightly crushed

Combine the water and sugar in a saucepan and heat until the sugar has dissolved, stirring periodically. Bring to a boil and immediately take off the heat. Place the ginger root in a heat-proof bowl, pour over the hot syrup mixture, and let steep until cool. Once cool, strain the mixture into a glass jar. Discard the ginger. Keep in the refrigerator for up to one month.

If you would like a spicier ginger syrup we suggest checking out Portland Syrups' Spicy Ginger Syrup for an extra kick.

Flame Heart

by Megan Fitzpatrick of JuneBaby

1 oz. bell pepper pickling vinegar

1 oz. tamarind syrup (see recipe at right)

1 oz. lemon juice

Combine all ingredients in a tumbler glass and fill with ice. Garnish with a lemon wheel.

Garnish: Lemon wheel

Glass: Lowball glass or tumbler

Feel free to swap out any pickling vinegar for the bell pepper, but be wary of anything with strong herb or garlic flavor.

Tamarind Syrup

20 grams tamarind paste

2 cups sugar

2 cups water

Break up the tamarind paste and add it to a pot with sugar and water. Simmer for about 15 minutes. For best results, pulse the cooled mixture in a Vitamix or Ninja blender for about 30 seconds. Strain through a mesh strainer.

Spiced Chai Apple

Cinnamon sugar
1 dash aromatic bitters
1 oz. Bright Chai Syrup by Portland Syrups
6 oz. DRY Fuji Apple Botanical Bubbly

Rim a lowball glass with cinnamon and sugar. Add ice, a dash of bitters, Bright Chai Syrup, and top with very cold DRY Fuji Apple Botanical Bubbly. Garnish with an apple slice.

Garnish: Apple slice

Glass: Lowball glass

Hibiscus Tea Cooler

by Jermaine Whitehead

2 oz. hibiscus tea shrub (see recipe at right)
Club soda

In a highball or Collins glass add ice and hibiscus tea shrub. Add club soda and stir. Garnish with raspberries and a fresh rosemary sprig.

Garnish: Raspberries and rosemary

Glass: Collins or highball glass

Hibiscus Tea Shrub

½ cup raspberries
½ cup dried hibiscus leaves
1 red chili (seeds removed and sliced)
2 cups white sugar
1 cup champagne vinegar

In a large canning jar combine the raspberries, hibiscus leaves, chili and sugar. Seal tightly and shake well to ensure that the sugar coats all of the fruit. Place the jar in the refrigerator for 2–3 days, shaking a few times a day until the fruit breaks down and becomes a syrup. Strain the mixture through a fine mesh sieve, pressing the solids with a wooden spoon to remove all of the liquid. Discard the solids.

Transfer the raspberry hibiscus syrup to a clean jar and add the champagne vinegar. Secure the lid and shake to combine. Store, sealed tightly, in the refrigerator for up to one month.

Watermelon DRY-rita

2 Tbsp. lime juice, plus a lime wedge
Hot Lava Sea Salt by Salty Wahine
4–6 cubes chilled fresh watermelon
Fresh mint
Several serrano chili slices
DRY Watermelon Botanical Bubbly, chilled

Run a slice of lime around the edge of a wine glass and dip into the Hot Lava Sea Salt, making sure the salt adheres to the rim.

In a blender, combine the fresh watermelon cubes and lime juice. Add the blended watermelon to a cocktail shaker with a few small slices of serrano chili and a few fresh mint leaves. Shake until combined, pour into the prepared glass, and top with DRY Watermelon Botanical Bubbly. Garnish with mint and a lime wheel.

Garnish: Mint and lime

Glass: Wine glass

Firecracker

1 oz. lime juice
1 sugar cube
Jalapeño slices to taste
Kosher salt
Cubed fresh watermelon
8 oz. DRY Watermelon Botanical Bubbly

Mix lime juice, sugar cube and jalapeño in a shaker, and let the cube dissolve. Add ice and shake until cold. Rim glass with salt, add watermelon cubes, and pour the shaker mixture into the glass. Top with DRY Watermelon Botanical Bubbly. Garnish with a lime wheel.

Garnish: Lime wheel

Glass: Collins glass

Smoke & Mirrors

by Jermaine Whitehead

3 oz. Harney and Sons Smoke Tea, chilled
1 oz. lemon juice
¾ oz. simple syrup (see recipe p. 52)
DRY Ginger Botanical Bubbly

Add Harney and Sons Smoke Tea, lemon juice and simple syrup to a cocktail shaker with ice. Shake hard for 15 seconds. Strain into a lowball glass filled with ice. Top with DRY Ginger Botanical Bubbly. Garnish with lemon peel.

Garnish: Lemon peel

Glass: Lowball glass

If you want to add a little drama to the presentation, garnish with a cinnamon stick with a burnt end. Simply use a kitchen torch to light a small portion of the cinnamon stick on fire. Gently blow out the flame and place on top of the glass.

Orange Saffron DRY-rita

2 orange slices
½ tsp. honey
1 oz. Blood Orange Saffron Shrub by Element
Shrub
1½ oz. Ritual Zero-Proof Tequila
Kosher salt
3 oz. DRY Blood Orange Botanical Bubbly

In a glass or shaker tin muddle two orange slices
and honey. Add Blood Orange Saffron Shrub and
Ritual Tequila and stir. Rim a rocks glass with salt,
add crushed ice to the glass and strain in the shaker
mixture. Top with DRY Blood Orange Botanical
Bubbly. Garnish with a slice of orange that has been
dipped in salt on one side.

Garnish: Salt-dipped orange slice

Glass: Rocks glass

DRY Pineapple Chili Limeade

Kosher salt, sugar, and chili powder for rim
Lime wedge
3–4 large fresh pineapple chunks
1 oz. lime juice
1 oz. Mango Habanero Syrup by Portland
*   Syrups*
Dash of chili powder
DRY Pineapple Botanical Bubbly, chilled

Mix equal parts salt, sugar and chili powder. Run a slice of lime around the edge of a lowball glass and dip into the salt-sugar-chili powder mixture. Blend or muddle the fresh pineapple chunks, lime juice, Mango Habanero Syrup and chili powder until smooth. Pour the entire mixture into the rimmed glass. Top with chilled DRY Pineapple Botanical Bubbly and garnish with a lime wheel and a dried chili.

Garnish: Lime wheel and dried chili

Glass: Lowball glass

Savory

Herbs & Soda

1–2 sprigs fresh herbs, like rosemary or thyme
Club soda or tonic

Smack a couple of sprigs of fresh herbs between
your hands, and add to a rocks glass filled with ice.
Top with soda or tonic.

Garnish: Herb sprigs

Glass: Rocks glass

*It's very important that you use fresh herbs
instead of dried, because fresh herbs
have essential oils that are released when
lightly muddled or smacked. Choose your
favorite herb based on your preference.
It's a deceptively simple drink, and utterly
refreshing.*

DRY & Dirty

1 oz. zero-proof gin
½ oz. olive brine
1 oz. lime juice
Dash of onion brine
DRY Cucumber Botanical Bubbly

In a shaker mix zero-proof gin, olive brine, lime juice, onion brine and ice. Shake until cold. Strain into a chilled martini glass and top with DRY Cucumber Botanical bubbly. Garnish with an olive or a pearl onion.

Garnish: Pearl onion or olive

Glass: Martini glass

Highlands Fog

Canned whipped cream
Fresh rosemary
4–6 oz. DRY Lavender Botanical Bubbly

In a Yarai mixing glass or pint glass, add two good squirts of whipped cream. Smack two sprigs of rosemary and add to the glass. Add ice and top with DRY Lavender Botanical Bubbly. Stir quickly to chill, and strain into a chilled coupe or martini glass. Garnish with sprigs of rosemary.

Garnish: Rosemary sprigs

Glass: Martini glass or coupe

Down to Earth Cold Brew

by Jermaine Whitehead

3 oz. Stumptown Cold Brew Coffee
¾ oz. mint syrup (see recipe below)
DRY Lavender Botanical Bubbly

Pour cold brew and mint syrup into a highball or Collins glass filled with ice. Mix well with a spoon. Top with DRY Lavender Botanical Bubbly. Garnish with sprigs of lavender and mint.

Garnish: Lavender and mint

Glass: Collins, highball or rocks glass

Mint Syrup

6–8 sprigs mint
16 oz. rich simple syrup (2 parts sugar
*   to 1 part water)*

Bring a small saucepan of water to a boil. Gather herb sprigs by the stems and plunge into the boiling water for 15 seconds. Remove herbs from boiling water and immediately submerge in a bowl of ice water for one minute. Pat dry on a clean kitchen towel. Remove the leaves and place them in a blender with simple syrup. Blend for one minute. Strain the syrup through a fine-mesh strainer and bottle. Keep refrigerated for up to 2 weeks.

Baby Temperance

by Erik Hakkinen of Roquette

½ oz. lemon juice

½ oz. lime juice

¼ oz. 5-spice syrup (see recipe at left)

3 oz. DRY Fuji Apple Botanical Bubbly

3 oz. DRY Ginger Botanical Bubbly

In a cocktail shaker add lemon juice, lime juice, 5-spice syrup and ice. Shake well and strain into a chilled Collins glass. Add 2 oz. each of DRY Fuji Apple Botanical Bubbly and DRY Ginger Botanical Bubbly to the glass. Add ice, top with remaining DRY Fuji Apple and DRY Ginger Botanical Bubbly, and garnish with a long lemon peel and straw. Add an extra star anise pod, if you have one, for an extra special garnish.

Garnish: Lemon peel and anise star

Glass: Collins glass

5-Spice Syrup

1 cup cane sugar

½ cup filtered water

½ tsp. ground 5-spice (1 full tsp. for strong flavor)

Heat water to boil in a saucepan, reduce heat to simmer, add sugar and 5-spice syrup, and stir constantly until all ingredients are incorporated. Let cool completely before using or refrigerating. Use within two weeks.

Autumn in Provence

by Amanda Reed

4 oz. DRY Cranberry Botanical Bubbly

1 oz. red verjus (verjus is the fresh juice from
   unripe wine grapes)

¾ oz. Herbs de Provence infused honey syrup
   (see recipe below)

½ oz. fresh lemon juice

Add ingredients to a wine glass and mix. Add ice.
Garnish with a sprig of fresh thyme or rosemary.

Garnish: Sprig of thyme or rosemary

Glass: Wine glass or rocks glass

Herbs de Provence Infused Honey Syrup

8 oz. honey

4 oz. hot water

½ oz. each: lavender, thyme, rosemary
   (all de-stemmed)

Add honey and water to a small pot, and heat until combined. Add herbs and infuse for 48 hours. Strain through a fine mesh strainer.

Cucumber Basil Collins

2 oz. lime juice
2–3 dashes bitters (optional)
Basil leaves
6 oz. DRY Cucumber Botanical Bubbly

In a shaker mix lime juice, bitters and torn basil leaves. Add ice. Shake until cold and the basil is bruised. Pour DRY Cucumber Botanical Bubbly over ice into a Collins glass, then add the lime and basil mix. Garnish with a lime wheel, basil leaf, and slice of cucumber.

Garnish: Lime wheel, basil leaf, cucumber slice

Glass: Collins glass

Beet It

by Jermaine Whitehead

2 oz. beet juice
1 oz. water
¾ oz. lemon juice
1 raspberry
¾ oz. ginger syrup (see recipe at right)
DRY Cucumber Botanical Bubbly

Add beet juice, water, lemon juice, raspberry, and ginger syrup into a cocktail shaker with ice. Shake hard for 10 seconds. Double strain into a highball or Collins glass. Top with DRY Cucumber Botanical Bubbly. Garnish with a cucumber peel.

Garnish: Cucumber peel

Glass: Collins or highball glass

Ginger Simple Syrup

1 cup sugar (white granulated)
¾ cup water
1 cup ginger root (sliced)

In a saucepan on medium heat, combine the sugar and water. Stir constantly until the sugar is dissolved. Add the ginger and continue to heat, bringing the syrup to a light boil.

Cover, reduce heat, and allow to simmer for about 15 minutes.

Remove from the heat and allow to steep in the covered pan for about 1 hour, or until it reaches your preferred taste. Strain using a fine mesh strainer, and bottle under a tight seal.

DRY Bloody Mary

Maple syrup
Kosher salt
Bacon bits
2–3 stems cilantro
6–8 oz. Bloody Mary mix
Tabasco sauce to taste
2–3 oz. DRY Cucumber Botanical Bubbly

Rim a Collins or highball glass by dipping the edge in maple syrup. Mix kosher salt and bacon bits, then dip the maple syrup-rimmed glass into the mixture. In a shaker or pint glass add ice, cilantro, Bloody Mary mix and Tabasco to taste, and shake. Pour into the rimmed glass and top with DRY Cucumber Botanical Bubbly. Garnish with a lime wedge, celery stalk, and pickle as desired.

Garnish: Lime, celery, pickle

Glass: Collins or highball glass

Juice Cleanse

by Megan Fitzpatrick of JuneBaby

2 oz. pepper-carrot juice (see recipe at right)

¾ oz. cucumber syrup (see recipe below)

½ oz. lime juice

⅛ oz. saline solution (5 parts water to 1 part salt)

Tajin seasoning

Combine ice, carrot juice, cucumber syrup, lime juice, and saline solution in a cocktail shaker and shake until cold. Dip half of the rim of your coupe glass in lime juice and then in Tajin seasoning. Strain the mixture into the coupe.

Garnish: None

Glass: Coupe

This is our cover cocktail! That's all. We just thought it was so pretty it deserved to be in the spotlight and we wanted you to know.

Pepper-Carrot Juice

1 dried Morita pepper

1 cup carrot juice

Warm the carrot juice on the stove over medium heat. Slice your dried Morita pepper and discard the stem. Any pepper with a little heat and smoky flavor will do, but Moritas are recommended. Steep in the carrot juice for 10–15 minutes. Remove from heat and strain.

Cucumber Syrup

½ a cucumber

1 cup sugar

1 cup water

Boil the water and combine with the sugar to make a simple syrup. Slice the cucumber and add to a blender with the syrup. Blend on high and strain through a mesh strainer.

The Guide to Zero-Proof Cocktails
DRY Soda Company

Founder and CEO
Sharelle Klaus

Chief Marketing Officer
Betsy Frost

Creative Director/Author
Kira Bottles

Art and Photography Director
Joska Borbely

Contributing Mixologists
Bridgett Bottles, Kira Bottles, Megan Fitzpatrick,
Erik Hakkinen, Amanda Reed, Jermaine Whitehead

Line Editor
Willa Konsmo

Copy Editor
Annie Brulé

Stylist
Callie Meyer

Stylist's Assistant
Dawnelle de Marco

Special Projects
WHY For Good

Published by Chatwin Books